Cashier

by Ann-Marie Kishel

first step nonfiction

Lerner Publications Company · Minneapolis

What does a cashier do?

She scans your things.

She takes your money.

He counts the money.

She uses the cash register.

He gives change.

Do you know a cashier?